Whether death comes to your loved one after a long and fruitful life or unexpectedly, by accident, it comes as a terrible shock. The purpose of this book is to help you during those first hours and days when you are struggling to comprehend and accept the emptiness in your life and in your heart. Bestselling author Charles L. Allen's reassuring presentation of the Easter message of resurrection and eternal life is complemented by sensitive verse by Helen Steiner Rice to comfort and strengthen you. This book comes to you with the prayer that it will bring real meaning and hope "when you lose a loved one."

BY Charles L. Allen

In Quest of God's Power
God's Psychiatry
The Touch of the Master's Hand
All Things Are Possible Through Prayer
When You Lose a Loved One
The Twenty-Third Psalm
Healing Words
The Life of Christ
Prayer Changes Things
The Sermon on the Mount
Life More Abundant
The Charles L. Allen Treasury
When You Graduate
The Miracle of Love
The Miracle of the Holy Spirit
What I Have Lived By
You Are Never Alone
Perfect Peace

When You Lose a Loved One

Charles L. Allen

With

Life Is Forever

Helen Steiner Rice

Fleming H. Revell Company
Old Tappan, New Jersey

Library of Congress Cataloging in Publication Data

Allen, Charles Livingstone, 1913–
  When you lose a loved one.

  1. Consolation.   I.   Rice, Helen Steiner. Life is
forever. 1980.   II.   Title.
BV4905.2.A4 1980   248'.86   79-24773
ISBN 0-8007-5031-4

Library of Congress Catalog Card Number: 59–5995

Scripture in *When You Lose a Loved One* is from the King James Version of the Bible.

The text of "You Need Not Fear Death" is from *In Quest of God's Power*, by Charles L. Allen. Published by Fleming H. Revell Company and copyrighted by them in 1952.

The text of "Christ in the Presence of Death" is from *The Touch of the Master's Hand*, by Charles L. Allen. Published by Fleming H. Revell Company and copyrighted by them in 1956.

Contents

You Need Not Fear Death   9
  Doorway to a Larger Life   15
  God Is the God He Is   17
  When a Loved One Has Died   19
  Death Is Not a Bad Experience   21
  Maybe Death Was a Blessing   23
  They Have Not Died   24
  Today in Paradise   26
  Be Inspired by Those Now Gone   31
  Life Must Go On   33
  We Never Lose Them   35
  Eternal Life Begins Now   37
  Die in Sin   38
  The Resurrection   40
  So Many Have Found It   42
  Our Lord's First Easter Message   44

Christ In the Presence of Death   49
  Lazarus Died   54
  Martha Still Believed   57
  For Those Who Want Life Instead of Death 60
  The Dead Shall Live   63

Contents

The Living Shall Never Die   66
We Will Know Each Other in Heaven   70
Why Didn't Jesus Tell Us More About
    Heaven?   73
He Was Still Lazarus on the Other Side   76

In memory of
Charles Simpson O'Neal
May 13, 1922–January 16, 1949
Son of
Dr. and Mrs. W. S. O'Neal
Douglasville, Georgia

You Need Not Fear Death

To BEGIN WITH, every one of us is interested in death, because we know that someday we are going to die. A lot of people are afraid of death, and their fear takes much of the joy out of living. Many refuse to think about it at all. But death is not a monster; it is our best friend, and if we could be convinced of that, life would be so much freer and happier.

Recently, I was visiting a dear old lady in the hospital. Through the years she had developed a marvelous Christian faith, and now, as the shades were swiftly being drawn for her, she said to me, "Dr. Allen, the Father's house is mighty attractive to me now." She has suffered much, and, instead of dreading death, she looks forward to it as the greatest blessing of her life. She is not the least bit afraid. On the contrary, as she is coming in sight of the other shore, there is a radiant joy in her heart.

One of the greatest scientists this world has ever produced is Thomas A. Edison. He was a very exact man and was never satisfied until he had the full and final truth. His statements were always based on proved facts. When Mr. Edison was dying, he was heard to whisper, "It is very beautiful over there."

Thomas A. Edison, a genuine scientist and scholar, would never have said that had it not been true. "It is very beautiful over there"—he was reporting what he saw.

As Robert Louis Stevenson came to his last moment on earth, he whispered, "If this is death, it is easy." Alfred Lord Tennyson was convinced that this life is the "dull side of death."

Of course, the best and surest testimony that we have is in the Book that is the truest and surest of all books. John had started with Christ as a very young man. He made a lot of mistakes, but through the years of his long life he had been faithful. Now he was exiled on the Island of Patmos—a foul place, where he was separated from those he loved and from the work so dear to his heart.

But there are always compensations for our sorrows and disappointments and, to compensate dear old patient John, God rolled back the curtain and let him look over to the other side. What a marvelous report he gave us!

And God shall wipe away all tears from their eyes; and there shall be no more death, neither sorrow, nor crying, neither shall there be any more pain: for the former things are passed away.

Revelation 21:4

After he had seen that, John was never afraid again. And on the basis of his sure testimony, no one of us should ever fear going to a place like that.

Of course, no person in his right mind wants to die. We should want very much to live. I can speak from experience here. One night a physician told me I was going to die, and for a time I believed it. I can testify that when you come face to face with death it is not bad. I can honestly say I was not the least bit afraid.

On the other hand, I very much wanted to live. I had a wife and baby and longed to stay with them. Also, I had just started in my life's work and I wanted to continue it. That night I prayed, "Lord, I am not afraid to die, yet I very much want to live."

It is good to want to live. On the other hand, we should never let the fear of death become a dark shadow over our lives, shutting out the sunshine of God's wonderful love.

Doorway to a Larger Life

Death is the doorway to a larger life. I can understand this well because about the hardest thing in the life of a minister is moving away from a church he has served. As pastor, you come to love the people very deeply. You baptize their babies, marry their young people, bury their loved ones. You visit the sick, comfort the sorrowing, and thrill with many who find Christ as their Saviour.

However, when it comes time to move, you think of the church to which you are going. When I came to Grace in Atlanta I hated to leave Thomson, where I had been the pastor for four years. But then I thought of being pastor of a great church on a main thoroughfare in a big city. As I thought of the much greater

opportunities, moving became a thrilling experience.

Death is like that. We hate to leave the associations and interests of this life, but then
there is a larger life waiting beyond! There is
.something glorious and joyful about it.

God Is the God He Is

We need not fear death, because God is the God He is. Think of how wise and tender God is. When He brought us into this world, He planned it so beautifully. Can you think of a better way to be born than into the bosom of a mother? God made mothers. And if God so planned our birth in such lovely fashion, we can rest assured that He has planned our entrance into the next world in some manner that will be good, and even wonderful.

A mother who had lost a baby said to me, "I am so worried thinking about who will take care of it." I assured her that just as God had planned for her to take care of the precious little one in this world, we could be certain that He had just as lovingly planned for her baby's care in His great and eternal house.

LOOK, GOD

Look, God, I have never spoken to you,
But now I want to say "How do you do."
You see, God, they told me you didn't exist.
And like a fool I believed all this.

Last night from a shell hole I saw your sky.
I figured right then they had told me a lie.
Had I taken time to see things you made,
I'd have known they weren't calling a spade a
    spade.

I wonder, God, if you'd shake my hand.
Somehow, I feel you will understand.
Funny, I had to come to this hellish place
Before I had time to see your face.

Well, I guess there isn't much more to say,
But I'm sure glad, God, I met you today.
I guess the zero hour will soon be here,
But I'm not afraid since I know you're near.

The signal, well God, I'll have to go.
I like you lots and I want you to know.
Look, now, this will be a horrible fight
Who knows, I may come to your house tonight.

Though I wasn't friendly to you before,
I wonder, God if you'd wait at the door.
Look, I'm crying. Me, shedding tears!
I wish I'd known you these many years.

Well, I have to go now, God, good-bye;
Strange, since I met you I'm not afraid to die.

When a Loved One Has Died

Here on this earth we are gathered together in families. Our loved ones become inexpressibly precious to us. We live in intimate associations. One gets so close to mother and father, wife or husband, sons and daughters, that they literally become a part of one's very life. Then comes a day when a strange change comes over one we love.

He is transformed before our very eyes. The light of life goes out of him. He cannot speak to us nor we to him. He is gone and we are left stunned and heartbroken. An emptiness and loneliness comes into our hearts. We brokenheartedly say, "That one whom I loved is dead." It is such a cold, hopeless thing to realize.

Then, out of the very depths of our despair,

like the melody of music coming from a mighty organ, like the refreshing sound of rippling waters, comes that marvelous declaration of our Lord:

I am the resurrection, and the life: he that believeth in me, though he were dead, yet shall he live: And whosoever liveth and believeth in me shall never die.

John 11:25, 26

Then we know! We *know* we have not lost our loved ones who have died. We have been separated, and so long as we live there will be an empty place left in our hearts. To some extent, the loneliness will always be there. But when we really know that one is not forever lost, it does take away the sorrow. There is a vast difference between precious memories, loneliness, the pain of separation, on the one hand, and a sorrow that ruins and blights our lives, on the other hand.

Death Is Not a Bad Experience

It is good to remember that death itself is not a bad experience. Some time ago there was an article in *McCall's* magazine entitled, "How Does It Feel to Die?" It was written by nine eminent physicians. The article quoted a statement by the famous Dr. William Osler, "Most human beings not only die like heroes, but, in my wide clinical experience, die really without pain or fear." All nine of the doctors agreed with that statement.

Dr. H. D. Van Fleet sums up the findings of all nine doctors. He says:

I use the word sweetness in connection with death. As a doctor who has seen many people expire, I know it is often sweet to die. Frequently I have seen a change of expression as the moment of death approached, almost a smile, before the last breath was taken. Science cannot explain this, as science cannot explain the dynamic power which controls life. What one may see at the point of death will probably remain an eternal mystery. But it should remain, too, a vision with no terrors for any of us.

A woman told me after a service recently that she could testify to the correctness of the above statement. She was out swimming in the ocean and was pulled under. She was in the very process of drowning, and almost did drown. But just before she lost consciousness, the one thought that filled her mind was this: "Mama will worry about me, but I wish she knew how easy it is."

When we realize that death was really an easy and happy experience for our loved one, that helps a lot.

Maybe Death Was a Blessing

A second thought that helps is that perhaps death was a blessing for our loved one. There are many things worse than death, and I rather think that, instead of becoming harsh and bitter when we have lost a loved one, we might better have faith in the goodness and mercy of God. Only God can know all the facts. Instead of hating God for letting some loved one die, we might later thank Him with all our heart.

They Have Not Died

Jesus said, "Whosoever liveth and believeth in me shall never die." Death is not the end, it is really the beginning of life. The Bible is a wonderful book. It is so gentle and kind. Through His Word, God tries to tell us something of the glories of the new life on the other side. But it is beyond our understanding. We just cannot imagine how wonderful that life really is. So we are told:

> Eye hath not seen, nor ear heard, neither have entered into the heart of man, the things which God hath prepared for them that love him.
>
> 1 Corinthians 2:9

People do not come back from the other side. Perhaps they cannot come back. On the other hand, perhaps they do not want to come back. Whatever life on the other side may be like, we can be sure our loved ones are enjoying a happier and larger life than they had on this side.

My own father died just after midnight in an Atlanta hospital. I loved him very deeply. He was a minister, and we were very close. I lived at Douglasville, about twenty-five miles from Atlanta, and early that morning I was driving home. A nauseating despondency had settled over me. But as I went over a hill I saw the sunrise in all its glory. Then I thought of that lovely song, "Sunrise tomorrow, sunrise tomorrow . . . sunrise with Jesus for eternity."

Then, like the dawn, a truth of tremendous import burst upon me. "Why, the sunrise has come for one whom I love." That very moment his passing became all right for me.

Arthur Brisbane pictured a crowd of grieving caterpillars carrying a dead cocoon to its final resting place. The poor, distressed caterpillars were weeping and heartbroken. But all the while the lovely butterfly fluttered happily over their heads!

Today in Paradise

The most hopeful and helpful words about life after death for me are the words Christ spoke to the penitent man who was dying that day by His side. "Today shalt thou be with me in paradise" (Luke 23:43). Here are three great affirmations:

Today . . . After Lazarus had died, Jesus said to Martha, "Thy brother shall rise again." But Martha replied, "I know that he shall rise again in the resurrection at the last day." She gets little comfort from the thought of a resurrection in some dim, distant future. Then Jesus replied:

> I am the resurrection, and the life: he that believeth in me, though he were dead, yet shall he live; And whosoever liveth and believeth in me shall never die.
>
> John 11:23–26

Jesus is saying that the resurrection comes immediately after death. Today—today—today.

Thou shalt be with me. . . . Thou—me. We will be the same people over there as we are here. Jesus said to Martha, "Thy brother shall rise again" (John 11:23). Even though he had passed on, he was *still* her brother.

After death, Jesus Himself had the same loving features and was recognized by those who had known Him. He had the same nail prints in His hands. He had the same love. He was the same beyond the grave as He was before the grave.

I know the fact of recognition after death presents difficulties, but without that assurance eternal life would mean very little. Before I was born, my mother and father had a little girl, Ruth, who died. Though the years came and went, they never completely gave up Ruth. Her little picture was on the mantle through the years. I think I know how they felt.

Some years ago my wife and I were separated from our oldest son for some weeks. We missed him very much and I will never forget the night we finally returned home. Somebody could have changed the doors and put in their stead doors made of pearl. The floors might have been overlaid with gold while we were gone. But we would not have noticed that. As we went into the house we wanted to see our baby, and, if he had not been there, no matter how fine the house might have been, it would not have been home for us.

And as my father entered the eternal city of God, I know it made no difference to him whether or not the gates were of pearl. He did not care whether the streets were of gold or concrete. What he wanted was to see his baby. And if his baby had not been there and if he had not known her, no matter what else might have been there, it would not have been heaven for him.

We will see our loved ones again.

In paradise. I think Jesus meant the same thing that we mean by heaven. I do not think there is an intermediary place. And what a glorious thing it is to think of what heaven is like. It is so grand and glorious that our small, finite minds cannot fully comprehend it. And, in fact, it means different things to different people.

There was Fanny Crosby. She was blind all her life and when she dreamed of heaven I think she wrote her finest song:

Some day the silver cord will break,
And I no more as now shall sing;
But O the joy when I shall wake,
Within the palace of the King.
And I shall *see* Him face to face.

It was for her a place where she could see.

As St. John looked into heaven, the first thing he saw was that "there was no more sea" (Revelation 21:1). He was exiled on Patmos. The sea was his prison. The sea kept him from doing what he wanted to do and being what he wanted to be. The sea was his handicap. In heaven there are no more handicaps.

After a service recently, a man who had lost both his hands in an accident asked me, "When I get to heaven will I have some hands?" That is what heaven means to him.

Last year I buried a beautiful young lady. That is, she was beautiful physically, but terribly handicapped mentally. Her mind never did develop, and after the service her mother, who loved her more than life itself, said, "I am so happy because now I know her handicap has been removed."

All of us have handicaps of some kind. There are things we want to do, but have not the ability or opportunity here to do them. But over there the handicaps will be taken away, and we will be able both to be and to do all on which our heart is set.

"Today shalt thou be with me in paradise." What a glorious and happy thought that is!

Be Inspired by Those Now Gone

One of our great American masterpieces is *Abraham Lincoln: The Prairie Years* by Carl Sandburg. In it he describes life on the great prairies of the Middle West during the pioneer days. Life was extremely hard for the pioneers, and their hands became gnarled, says Sandburg, "like the roots of the oak tree."

Medical resources were meager, and sickness and death were their ever-present enemies. One-fourth of all their babies died. Malaria and milk sickness were plagues that killed thousands. Nancy Hanks, Lincoln's own mother, died of milk sickness, as did one of his sisters and her baby.

Sandburg tells about those difficult days, but also he tells how on the Lord's day they would go to the crude churches they had built to hear some pioneer, circuit-riding preacher and sing together:

There's a land that is fairer than day,
And by faith we can see it afar;
For the Father waits over the way,
To prepare us a dwelling place there.

And he declares that was the faith that kept them going, that built America and made America great.

Life Must Go On

The last time I was in Mobile I went around to see a friend whom I appreciate and admire very much, George Downing. After George finished Emory, he went with the Coca-Cola Company and made an outstanding record. At the close of the war he was sent to Europe in a responsible position. He went ahead and got a place to live, then his lovely young wife and their two precious little girls took seats on a plane to join him. But on the way over the airplane crashed into a mountain, and, along with a number of others, they perished.

We held a simple memorial service for them, and in the days following George and I were together a lot. I wanted to do something for him, but he did far more for me. Not one word of bitterness did he ever speak. In no way did he become harsh or ugly. His heart was broken, but his spirit was magnificent.

We lived at Thomson, Georgia, and at the time we were building a new Sunday-school building. One day George said, "I would like to furnish the nursery, kindergarten, and primary rooms in memory of those I love." He went on to tell how much Sunday school had meant to his little girls, and now that they were in the Father's house above he wanted to do something in the Father's house here on earth which would be an inspiration to other little girls and boys.

He bought a lot of things—small chairs and tables, a tiny organ and a little piano, toys of all kinds, a record player and a library of records, books children would like, and lovely pictures for the walls.

Now George is married again, and they have a little baby. He is working, he is happy, he is living a great life. And that is just as it should be. Sorrows and disappointments come, more to some than to others, but to some extent to everyone. But out of the sorrows come lovely and beautiful things. Those we have lost inspire us to grander and nobler living; and, instead of becoming bitter, we become better. And life goes on.

We Never Lose Them

I used to play baseball, and my father went to the games because he was always interested in whatever his children did. I remember one game especially. It was a tight game, and I happened to get a long hit. I was running around the bases as fast as I could, but I seemed to gain added strength when I heard him shouting above the crowd, "Come on home, Charles, come on home." Since he has been gone, there have been times when the going was a little harder for me and I have been tempted to do less than my best, but then I could hear him saying, "Come on home, Charles, come on home."

The pull of a loved one who is now in the home above often is our very strongest influence.

Florence Jones Hadley has said it beautifully
in her poem:

I think ofttimes as the night draws nigh
Of an old house on the hill,
Of a yard all wide and blossom-starred
Where the children played at will.
And when at last the night came down,
Hushing their merry din,
Mother would look around and ask,
 "Are all the children in?"

'Tis many and many a year since then,
And the old house on the hill
No longer echoes to childish feet
And the yard is now so still.
But I see it all, as the shadows creep,
And though many the years have been,
I still can hear my mother ask,
 "Are all the children in?"

I wonder if when the shadows fall
On the last, short earthly day,
When we say good-by to the world outside,
All tired with our childish play;
When we step out into that other land
Where mother so long has been,
Will we hear her ask, just as of old,
 "Are all the children in?"

Eternal Life Begins Now

Many people are walking around on this earth who are dead or partly dead. Their hopes are dead. Their dreams and ideals are dead. Someone once wrote a poem about a wild duck. He could fly high and far, but one day he landed in a barnyard. There life was less exciting but easier. The duck began to eat and live with the tame ducks and gradually he forgot how to fly. He became fat and lazy.

In the spring and fall, however, as the wild ducks flew overhead, something stirred inside him, but he could not rise to join them. The poem ends with these lines:

He's a pretty good duck for the shape he's
  in,
But he isn't the duck that he might have
  been.

Die in Sin

The great prophet Ezekiel told us long ago that "the soul that sinneth, it shall die" (18:4). St. Paul warned us that "the wages of sin is death" (Romans 6:23). The most tragic death is not physical death. It is the death of the soul, the death of the personality, the dying of something fine inside one.

We need only to remember the story of Belshazzar the night of his great feast. In his drunken stupor Belshazzar "commanded to bring the golden and silver vessels which his father Nebuchadnezzar had taken out of the temple which was in Jerusalem; that the king and the princes might drink therein."

Even in his wildest moments, Nebuchadnezzar had not dared to lay his profane hands on the sacred vessels from the temple of the eternal God, but his godless son did it and that night a hand appeared and wrote on the wall, "Mene, mene, tekel, u-pharsin." The king's face went white. He was scared into soberness, and he immediately sent for the preacher. He had not wanted the preacher around before, but now he needed him. Daniel translated the words on the wall for him:

Thou art weighed in the balances, and art found wanting.

Daniel 5:27

Many people have desecrated the high and holy things in their lives, and, little by little, have died until—on God's side of the scales—there is little left.

The Resurrection

But listen to these glorious words of our Lord:

> I am the resurrection, and the life: he that believeth in me, though he were dead, yet shall he live.

In Korea they call a Christian a "resurrected" person. They mean that the soul of the Christian was spiritually dead, but he has allowed the spirit of Christ to come in, believed in Him, responded to that belief, and has begun to live again.

Once they were building a new highway in England. In the way stood a very, very old building. The workmen tore it down and cleared off the ground on which it stood. After the ground had been exposed to the sunshine and rain for some months, a wonderful thing happened. Flowers began to spring up, and botanists and naturalists from all over England came to study them. Many of the flowers were identified as plants the Romans had brought to England almost two thousand years before. Some of the plants that sprang up are completely unknown today.

Hidden there in the ground, without air and light, the seeds seemed to have died. But they were not dead. As soon as the obstacles were cleared away, and the sunshine let in, they sprang into the fulness of their beauty.

So the seeds of eternal life are in every human life. But often those seeds are buried under such things as unbelief, selfishness, pride, lust, preoccupation, or some other sin. But when in humility and with childlike faith we bow before Him, it is the resurrection and the life for us. Marvelous things happen within our souls and we become finer and better than ever we had dared to hope. Life takes on for us a new meaning, a new radiance and beauty, a new happiness, and peace becomes ours. We live again.

So Many Have Found It

Some time ago, when it was announced that I was to preach in a series of revival services in a certain town in another state, I received a letter from a couple living there inviting, even insisting, that I stay in their home. I was surprised, because when I was their pastor in other years they had had little use or time for me. Life had become too tame for them at that time, and they began doing a lot of things that were wrong. Little by little they had let their highest ideals and dreams die. They had stopped coming to church.

When I arrived they greeted me with the very warmest cordiality. They gave me the nicest room in the house, there were lovely flowers on the dresser and a luscious basket of fruit on the table. Everything they could possibly do for my comfort they did. She even insisted on serving my breakfast in my room for my convenience.

They had not been attending church, but they both went that night. At the close of the service, as I always do in revivals, I gave a call for prayer at the altar. This couple came. They lingered longer than any others. I watched them, and I could tell it was not easy, but there that night at the altar they prayed through. I was with them the rest of that week, and have seen them many times since. Being well acquainted with them, I know that once they had died, and then had risen again. A new life is now theirs, a new joy and a new peace.

It was not me they wanted to honor in their home that week. They had simply come to see that the things they had sneered at and turned their backs on in years gone by were the things that really mattered most. They wanted to get back what they had lost, and they did.

I see that same thing happen every Sunday night as hundreds of people pray at the altar of Grace Church. Hundreds have told me after our night service that they had been lost and now were found; once were dead but now are alive.

Life—eternal life—is here, right now, for all who will accept it.

Our Lord's First Easter Message

Above all things, do not miss our Lord's first Easter message. According to St. Mark 16:7, it was, "Go . . . tell his disciples and Peter. . . . "

Tell His disciples! Those who ran away when He was arrested. Who made no protest at His trial. The disciples who quit and went back fishing. Who were not loyal when they were needed so badly.

Yes, and tell all His disciples today who once started with Him but found the going hard and gave up and quit. Tell those who have turned their backs on the better way, who have lowered their standards and have shamefully failed. Tell those who have lost their inspiration to live their best, those who have lost their hope and whose lives have been shattered. Tell every person who would like to try again that Jesus is risen and there is a new chance.

Among the disciples was "doubting" Thomas. He had become confused in his thinking, had lost his faith, and could not accept the testimony of others.

Yes, and tell those who have difficulty in believing. Whose faith is a bit shaky and whose doubts are very real. Tell them that Jesus is not angry because of their doubts. Instead, He comes tenderly and sympathetically to restore faith and bring certainty. He wants it told to all who doubt that He is risen.

" . . . and Peter," He said. I am so glad He named Peter. The disciple who promised that though all others would forsake Christ, he would remain loyal. Yet at the very moment Christ was on trial Peter stood by the fire "warming himself." His own comforts he put above his loyalty to Christ. He broke his promise. Yet Jesus especially wanted Peter to know He had risen; that He was ever ready to forget the past and give Peter a new chance.

Yes, tell every person who started but for some reason quit. Tell those who made promises but broke them. Tell every person who has failed, who has sinned, who would receive forgiveness, that the Christ of the second chance is here and ready to start with him again.

Yes, and tell all those who have difficulty in accepting a future life. Tell them that Christ is risen and that He said, ". . . because I live, ye shall live also" (John 14:19). Also that He said, "Whosoever liveth and believeth in me shall never die" (John 11:26).

The Easter message robs death of its terror and promises a solution to life's mysteries. The great Beethoven became deaf and could not hear his own music. However, he declared, "It is the hope of immortality with its brighter future that inspires me to keep on trying."

And Beethoven's biographer wrote, "With the shadows of the dark valley closing around him, he could look to the Land of Promise beyond, and with a mighty triumph sing of the joy and victory which surely awaited him in a world where the wrongs of earth are righted at last."

Why did that baby die, or that young husband get killed, or any of the great disappointments of life have to be? I do not know the answer, but because of Easter I do know there is an answer and that someday it will all be made plain.

Finally, the assurance of eternity is our greatest incentive to a life of consecrated service.

James Chalmers, after twenty-one hard years as a missionary, said:

> Recall the twenty-one years, give me back its shipwrecks, its standings in the face of death, the savages knocking me to the ground and beating me with clubs, give it back to me and I will still be your missionary.

Christ In the Presence of Death

I GET A NEW thrill every time I read the story of Jesus and Lazarus. It has love, pathos, drama, and builds up to a climax so grand that it includes both earth and heaven. It begins with Lazarus, who was sick. So many of the stories in the life of Christ begin with the needs of some person. In truth, that is where most of us begin with Christ. We have a need we cannot meet and we then look to Him who is able to supply our every need.

The two sisters, Mary and Martha, sent word to Him, saying, "Lord, behold, he whom thou lovest is sick." What a marvelous lesson in prayer! First, when trouble came, they wanted Christ to know about it. And through the centuries as unnumbered multitudes of people have become frightened or burdened, they have instinctively reached through the darkness to feel for the hand of Christ. We know He will be concerned.

My heart is stirred daily as I get letters from people I have never seen telling me their trou-

bles. The only contact many of these ever had
with me is reading my articles in a big met-
ropolitan newspaper. But their hearts have become burdened and they had no one to tell it
to who really cared. I read those letters with a
special prayer in my heart.

Mary and Martha were also showing a marvelous faith. They had a great need—they told
Christ about it—they felt that was sufficient.
They did not feel it necessary to tell Him what
to do. They had faith to believe that He would
do the right thing. In our prayers we would do
well to have as much faith. "He whom thou
lovest is sick." A short prayer, yet it contains
all that is necessary.

Now notice Christ's strange reaction to their
prayer. As you read the Gospels, you are impressed with His eagerness to help those who
came for His help. He was never too busy. No
person was ever turned away. So when the
word came about Lazarus, you might expect to
read how He hurried to Bethany to the bedside of Lazarus. Or better still, He might just
have spoken the word as He did on behalf of
the centurion's servant, and healed Lazarus at
the very moment. So we are surprised to read,

"He abode two days still in the same place where he was."

I can picture those two anxious sisters. They kept walking to and fro from the bedside of their loved to the window. "Why doesn't He come?" they would wonder in anguish. "Surely He will be here any moment now," one would say to comfort the other. But darkness came and He wasn't there. All through the night they watched and waited but still He didn't come. Another day slowly dragged by and still another night. Finally Lazarus died, and still He hadn't come.

That is the hardest part of prayer. If God says "No," we can accept it. If He says "Yes," we are glad. But when God keeps saying "Wait," we find that hardest to bear. And sometimes it does seem that God waits too long. But He doesn't. The old prophet was right when he said:

> For still the vision awaits its time. . . .
> If it seem slow, wait for it; it will surely
> come, it will not delay.
>
> Habakkuk 2:3, RSV

Lazarus Died

Why did Christ allow Lazarus to die? If we can answer that, maybe it will give us the answer to why God has allowed some of the pain, sorrow and suffering that you have come to bear. Recently I have been praying especially for a dear lady suffering day and night with arthritis. Why is God delaying the answer?

Certainly Christ knew about Lazarus' being sick. Also He knew of the worry and anguish in the heart of Mary and Martha. Sometimes we think God is not aware of our sorrows and needs. We may doubt that He even hears our prayers. But Jesus assures us that God even notes the fall of one little sparrow. Jesus knew of the seriousness of Lazarus' condition, yet He did nothing about it. Why?

It was not because He was unable to heal Lazarus. As you study His life you see He was able to heal even lepers, to make the cripple walk, the deaf hear and the blind see. Even the winds and waves obeyed His voice. We sometimes doubt God's ability to meet our particular situation. Thus we cease to pray and to look to Him. But God is always sufficient. With just one word Christ could have saved Lazarus. Why didn't He do it?

Sometimes we believe that our suffering is a sign that God is angry with us and wants to punish us. We may doubt His love for us. But such was not the case with Lazarus. The story begins with the love of Christ for him. "He whom thou lovest is sick," they said. And it has seemed to me that some who have suffered the most have been those who loved God the most. Notice the story says, "Now Jesus loved Martha, and her sister, and Lazarus."

He loved them, not as a family, but one by one. We must remember that God's love is always an individual love. Jesus was constantly dealing with the one person. Some of His greatest utterances were to individuals. He healed one by one. We talk about "mass" evangelism, but He talked about the shepherd going out after the one sheep. He loved this

[55]

one man who was sick. Then why did He let him die?

I don't know. I just do not know. I say with St. Paul, "For now we see through a glass, darkly." But I also say with Paul, "but then face to face: now I know in part; but then shall I know even as also I am known" (1 Corinthians 13:12). If we knew all the answers, we would not need faith. Faith takes up where sight leaves off. The Bible says, "Now faith is . . . the evidence of things not seen" (Hebrews 11:1). Faith pierces the darkness in our hearts and knows there is an answer, a reason—a good reason—and it accepts that fact and keeps moving toward God.

Lazarus did die. Then we read, "Many of the Jews came to Martha and Mary, to comfort them." So many things on this earth have changed—the clothes we wear, the food we eat, even the language we speak—but people are still the same. When a heart is broken, friends still come to sympathize, to comfort. And what a blessing it is to have someone to share our sorrows. Sometimes a friend who cares means more than anything else on earth.

Martha Still Believed

When Jesus finally came to Bethany where Lazarus died, we read that "Martha, as soon as she heard that Jesus was coming, went and met him." That is wonderful. While her brother was sick she had sent word to Christ and had expected Him to do something. Instead, He delayed coming until it seemed it was now too late. Death had beat Him there. Yet in spite of that Martha was not bitter.

She might have said, "I refuse ever to speak to Christ again. He failed me when I asked His help." But be it to her everlasting glory, she didn't say that. In my years as a minister I have come to know people in almost every condition. Many will bring tears of sympathy to your eyes. But the most pitiful, hopeless creature I have ever met is one who has allowed a sorrow to make him bitter. I am praying for a man now who said to me, "God could have saved me from this. He didn't and I will never darken the door of a church again."

Not only did Jesus fail to save Lazarus, He didn't even come to the funeral. He was their best friend. He could have come but He didn't. Their neighbors came. They sent flowers. They helped in every way they could. But Jesus didn't come. Still Martha was so anxious to see Him that she ran out to meet Him. We love her for that spirit.

Her first words to Him were: "Lord, If thou hadst been here, my brother had not died." Many times we feel that our troubles do come because God is not with us. Many couples can say, "Lord, if thou hadst been in our home, it would not have been broken." Many defeated, miserable people can say, "Lord, if thou hadst been in my life, things would have been different." But in cases like that, the reason for His absence may be that we refuse to let Him come in. God never forsakes us. We forsake Him.

Now notice the complete faith of Martha: ". . . even now, whatsoever thou wilt ask of God, God will give it to thee." It is so easy to lose hope and throw up our hands in despair. But we need to know that with Christ no person is hopeless. With Christ there is a solution to every problem. With Christ something can always be done. We only become hopeless when we refuse to believe.

Every Sunday night I ask my congregation to sing the little chorus: "Only believe, only believe; all things are possible, only believe." God's power in our lives is limited only by our lack of belief. What is your situation? Remember the faith of Martha—even when death had come, she still believed Christ could do something. We have a saying, "Where there is life, there is hope," but Martha goes even beyond that. She had hope even in death. At least we do have life and we should know that no matter what has happened, when we pray it will bring results.

Jesus said to her, "Thy brother shall rise again." To you He will say, There is still life ahead. May we rise to that faith.

For Those Who
Want Life
Instead of Death

Martha's heart was broken because of the death of her brother Lazarus. Jesus did declare, "Thy brother shall rise again," but that gave her very little comfort. She said, "I know that he shall rise again in the resurrection at the last day," but to her that was so far away. And the final resurrection seems so strange and vague.

Then Jesus said to her the most beautiful and comforting word that has ever been spoken in the presence of death:

I am the resurrection, and the life: he that believeth in me, though he were dead, yet shall he live: And whosoever liveth and believeth in me shall never die.

To comment on those words of our Lord is like trying to describe a rainbow or a sunset. Human words are so inadequate. You can't describe in words the sound of a gentle breeze rustling through the trees on a hot summer day, or the melody of a pipe organ, or the beauty of a rose, or the depth of a mother's love. In those words Christ reveals the glorious truth that it is possible for a human being to be forever beyond the reach of death.

Suppose some physician were to make a discovery that would put every person beyond the reach of cancer. The news would be proclaimed joyously around the world. Think about how that announcement would immediately take so much fear and dread out of our minds. I have talked with many people who suspected they might have cancer. The very suspicion so filled them with fear that they would not go to a doctor. I have seen others just give up and die when they learned they had cancer. The cancer did not kill them. Just the fear of it was enough.

And there are people who can hardly stand to hear the word death spoken. They live in such mortal dread of it that even the life they have is no joy. But the Son of God has come to tell us that death can be eliminated, and vast multitudes believe what He said. Why do we crowd our churches on Easter? We talk about the Easter parade, but new clothes are not the answer. On that day we come to church in large numbers because from Christ we have the assurance that death has been conquered.

A minister was talking to me about the competition of television with the church on Sunday night. At the church hour, a program comes out of New York that costs $60,000 to put on. The people can sit in their homes and see it. No church has that much money to spend on a single service.

Yet, he pointed out, the church does compete—not because it has more money to spend, but rather because it has something more valuable to offer. In the field of entertainment the church is left far behind, but in having a Christ who is the answer to death the church stands before thirsty people like a cool spring in the midst of a desert. As long as people desire life instead of death, they will come to Christ.

The Dead Shall Live

Jesus said to Martha, "I am the resurrection, and the life: he that believeth in me, though he were dead, yet shall he live: And whosoever liveth and believeth in me shall never die." There He is saying two things: (1) the dead shall live again; (2) the living shall never die.

"Though he were dead," our Lord said. There is such a thing as death. There are numbers of people walking the streets of any city who are dead. Do you remember when you were in your youth? Life was thrilling, songs and laughter filled your mind, you had high purposes and lofty ambitions. You were gloriously alive.

Little by little, however, as you grew older you settled down. Setbacks and disappointments came along. There was the old daily routine and the struggle to make a living. The very monotony of a lot of people's existence is a deadening thing. Before we realize it, we find ourselves in a rut. You know what a rut is? It is a grave with the ends knocked out—an endless grave. A lot of people are now buried in some rut.

Hopes can die, dreams can die, ideals can die. We remember the Bible tells us, "The soul that sinneth, it shall die" (Ezekiel 18:4). St. Paul warned that "The wages of sin is death" (Romans 6:23). We have a way of telling ourselves that a little sin doesn't hurt. We soothe and ease our conscience and we are told, "Don't worry about it." But let us never forget that sin and wrong can bring death inside of us. Then we become bodies without souls.

Study history and you will find that no civilization has ever been destroyed by an invading army or an outside enemy. But civilizations have died from the inside. Read again the story of Babylon. The city was so well fortified that no enemy could attack it. In the vaults were gold and silver and precious jewels beyond calculation. The people there felt safe and secure. But Babylon had lost its moral fiber; it leveled out the high and holy places and nothing remained sacred. When that happens either to a nation or to a person, it brings death. During the last war when France surrendered, Churchill said, "England has lost her buildings but France has lost her soul." And there are people who are getting along pretty well financially whose souls have died.

Even for those Christ is sufficient. "He that believeth in me, though he were dead, yet shall he live." Accepting Christ as a Saviour is not some little moral reform, it is a new birth and a new life.

The Living Shall Never Die

Jesus said, "Whosoever liveth and believeth in me shall never die." That is the most glorious promise ever made to humanity. We go to the cemetery. It is a sacred spot which we bathe with our tears, but our loved are not there. They never have been there. They never will be there. You bury only things that are dead, and Christ assures us that through Him we will never die. The body dies and is buried. The person does not die and therefore is not buried.

We remember the words of our Lord to the man dying by His side that day. He said:

Today shalt thou be with me in paradise.

Luke 23:43

Not in some dim, distant future—today. Not at some general resurrection—today. Not when some Gabriel blows a horn—today. Our life will not cease and start over again. It continues on in another place. The very moment we leave this body we begin living in the next life.

When I conduct a funeral I usually say to the family that it is both a time of sadness and rejoicing. When a loved one's body dies it breaks our hearts and fills our eyes with tears. We would not have it otherwise. There is something wrong with a person who can be physically separated from one he truly loved and not feel deep sorrow. It always leaves a hurt in our hearts that will never be healed. Sorrow because of death is not a lack of faith. Though we have complete confidence in the future life, still the separation is hard to bear.

Have you ever been on a college campus on the opening day of school? Proudly the parents drive up with their boy or girl. They help get the things to the room and are happy to see their child entering college and a larger life. But if you watch, you will see a mama quickly wipe some tears away when she thinks no one is looking. Even papa feels a little moisture in his eyes as he tells his child good-by. It is both a time of sadness and of joy.

Certainly one of the happiest occasions of all is a wedding. We want our children to marry, but it is a rare mother who doesn't shed some tears even though it is a happy time. We want our children to go away to college and to marry, but the separation comes hard. And to a much greater extent is that true when a loved one enters the Father's House. We do believe and we are confident they have entered a better life. But even that assurance does not keep us from feeling lonely without the physical presence of one we love.

After Jesus had given the assurance to Martha of life eternal, we read that she went to her heartbroken sister and told her, "The Master is come, and calleth for thee." He was not impatient with her sorrow. Instead, He comes to help. I frequently suggest to those in sorrow that they get away from other people and quietly think and pray for a little while. Many people have told me that in that time they

have felt the presence of God in a more defi-
nite way than ever before.

Above and beyond all things else, in time of
sorrow over the passing of a loved one, we
should come to love and appreciate Christ the
most. The story says Mary "arose quickly, and
came unto him." Surely to the One and only
One who can assure eternal life for our loved
ones and ourselves we should all want to come
quickly—without further delay.

We Will Know Each Other in Heaven

In company with Mary, Martha and a large number of other people, Jesus makes His way out to the cemetery where Lazarus was buried. Now we come to John 11:35, one of the most sublime verses in all the Bible. It contains only two words, but one could spend a long time considering the meaning of those two words: "Jesus wept." Why did He weep?

I once prepared a sermon on "The Sympathy of Christ" and I used those words as my text. It is certainly true that He understands our sorrows and enters into them with us. I still preach that sermon, but I had to get another text. Jesus did not weep over the death of Lazarus, because He knew that in a few moments Lazarus would be living again on this earth. Christ did not weep in sympathy with the sorrow of His friends, because in the raising of Lazarus their sorrow would be turned to joy.

I think the reason Christ wept that day was not because of the death of Lazarus, but rather because He felt it necessary to bring Lazarus back again to this earthly life.

In one of my pastorates there lived one of the godliest women I have ever known. I visited her often and her sure and certain faith was a strengthening force in my own life. Especially was I impressed with her power in prayer and she was a great help to me in learning how to pray. Often when I had special requests for prayer I would go to her and we would pray together. Always I noted how careful she was to close her prayer asking God not to grant our request unless it was best.

One day I asked her why she was so careful at that point. She told me the story of her husband. He had a heart attack. The doctor came and did all he could but it was a losing battle. The doctor was listening to his heart and then quietly said, "He is gone." The children became almost hysterical and said, "Mama, pray, Mama, pray." Quickly she knelt and

said, "Lord, bring him back to life." He
opened his eyes, his breathing became regu-
lar, he lived for nine years more. But those
nine years were for him so painful and un-
happy that no less than a thousand times did
she regret that God answered her prayer.

Often when someone dies we think how
much better it would have been if that one
could have lived. But we are not sure about
that. Before we make up our minds or become
bitter about some death, let us remember that
we do not know all the facts. As the old song
tells us:

Not now, but in the coming years,
It may be in the better land:
We'll read the meaning of our tears,
And there, some time, we'll understand.

For a loved one to die is a heartbreaking
experience. But for that one to live might be
worse, very much worse. Who but God really
knows? Thus let us not judge God until all
facts are before us.

Why Didn't Jesus Tell Us More About Heaven?

If we knew about the future life as Christ did, I am sure we would rejoice when our loved ones entered into it. Surely no one of us would be so selfishly cruel as to call one back from the City of God to the limitations and pains of this life.

That brings the question, Why did not Jesus tell us more about heaven? In the first place, there are no words in any language which can convey a true picture of the next life. Suppose you had the opportunity to talk with someone before he was born. Could you tell him what this life is like? Could you make a blind man understand what a sunset looks like? Could you tell a deaf man what great music sounds like?

St. Paul faced this situation and admitted

our utter inability to understand the next life. He said:

> Eye hath not seen, nor ear heard, neither have entered into the heart of man, the things which God hath prepared for them that love him.
>
> 1 Corinthians 2:9

I have often wondered why those who came back from the grave did not tell their experiences. I think the answer is they could not because of the total limitations of our language and understanding.

Another reason why I think Jesus did not tell us more about heaven is that it would have utterly spoiled this life for us. I remember how long and dull the days before Christmas were when I was a child. Along in October I would begin looking at the mail-order catalogue and making up a list of all the things I was going to get. It was hard to wait for that blessed morning when Santa Claus would come.

Suppose you call your child to dinner. On his plate are spinach, carrots, meat and the other things he should eat. Then sitting beside his plate is a beautiful strawberry shortcake, covered with whipped cream. It's mighty hard to eat spinach with strawberry shortcake right before you. In fact, most children can't do it.

And if Christ had put the picture of heaven within our hearts and in our sight, could we bear to live on this earth? Knowing that other life, would it not cause us to weep even more to call one of our loved ones back to this life? Surely death is not a monster to be feared. It is the greatest blessing God has prepared for us.

But Christ felt it necessary to call Lazarus back. So He said to those sisters, "Take ye away the stone." He could have moved that stone with just a word. Instead, He required them to use their strength. God's miracles are not for the lazy. We must use our strength and do our part and then He does the rest. Prayer is never a substitute for the sweat of your brow.

Now notice that Christ says, "Father, I thank thee that thou hast heard me." What a marvelous lesson in prayer! We quickly come to ask, but how rarely do we come back to God to thank Him for hearing.

He Was Still Lazarus on the Other Side

At the grave Jesus said, "Lazarus, come forth." Those words reveal to us three great truths concerning life after death:

(1) Lazarus was living independently of the physical body he had on earth. That means that our physical bodies are not essential to our continued life. St. Paul clearly points out that "flesh and blood cannot inherit the kingdom of God." Our bodies go back to dust. Death means that we are released from this body we now have and we are given a spiritual body which will not be under the physical laws our present bodies are. (Read 1 Corinthians 15.)

A mother whose baby had died asked me if the child will grow up in heaven. Certainly there is growth in heaven, but since we have spiritual bodies there we do not experience the physical growth we know here. After the death of his son, Calvin Coolidge inscribed on the flyleaf of a book these words: "To Edward K. Hall, in recollection of his son and my son, who have the privilege by the grace of God to be boys through all eternity."

(2) Those on the other side can hear those on this side. When Jesus called, Lazarus heard. I strongly believe there have been communications between people on each side of the grave. Heaven is not nearly so far away as we might suppose.

(3) Though our bodies are different, we are the same people on the other side as we are on this side. Jesus said, "Lazarus." Though he had died, he was still Lazarus. He said, "Thy brother shall rise again." He was their brother on this side; he was still their brother on the other side. At home you may have a little one that you think of as "my child," and you are right. But you are just as right to think of that one of yours who may be in the Father's House as "my child."

On the authority of Christ, there is not the slightest doubt but that we will see and know and love each other again. This fact disturbed some people to the point that they asked Christ, if people should marry several times, whose wife or husband would they be in the next life. He replied:

> In the resurrection they neither marry, nor are given in marriage, but are as the angels of God in heaven.
>
> Matthew 22:30

Marriage is a physical relationship and in heaven we will have spiritual bodies. The problems we think of in regard to the next life have all been worked out by God. We can trust Him to provide the right answers.

The important thing for us to know is that there is another life which is within the reach of every one of us. He said, "I am the resurrection, and the life: he that believeth in me, though he were dead, yet shall he live: And whosoever liveth and believeth in me shall never die." Then He added, "Believest thou this?" If you believe it, you will put your faith in Him as your Saviour and Lord.

Life Is Forever

BY Helen Steiner Rice

Everyone Needs Someone
A Gift of Love
Heart Gifts From Helen Steiner Rice
In the Vineyard of the Lord
Life Is Forever
Lovingly, Helen Steiner Rice
Loving Promises
Prayerfully
Somebody Loves You
Someone Cares

Life Is Forever

Helen Steiner Rice

GOD is LIFE
    and DEATH is the WAY
Man reaches the land
    of ETERNAL DAY!

Library of Congress Cataloging in Publication Data

Allen, Charles Livingstone, 1913–
  When you lose a loved one.

  1. Consolation.   I. Rice, Helen Steiner. Life is
forever. 1980.   II. Title.
BV4905.2.A4 1980   248'.86   79-24773
ISBN 0-8007-5031-4

Contents

A Personal Letter From the Author 85
Nothing on Earth Is Forever Yours—
      Only the Love of the Lord Endures! 89
Life Is Forever: Death Is a Dream! 91
I Do Not Go Alone 92
Spring Awakens What Autumn Puts to Sleep 93
Death Is a Doorway 94
There's Always a Springtime 95
"Because He Lives . . . We, Too, Shall Live" 97
When I Must Leave You 99
Each Spring, God Renews His Promise 101
Death Is Only a Part of Life 103
On the Other Side of Death 105
Death Opens the Door to Life Evermore 107
Life Is Eternal 109
"In Him We Live and Move and Have
      Our Being" 110
In God's Tomorrow There Is Eternal Spring 111
God Needed an Angel in Heaven 112
The Tiny "Rosebud"
      God Picked to Bloom in Heaven 113
Mothers Never Die—
      They Just Keep House up in the Sky 115
"Why Should He Die for Such as I?" 117
"I Know That My Redeemer Liveth" 119
All Nature Proclaims Eternal Life 120
"I Am the Way, the Truth, and the Life" 121

Contents

The Legend of the Raindrop 122

As Long As You Live and Remember—
Your Loved One Lives in Your Heart 124

A Consolation Meditation 125

In the Hands of God Even Death
Is a Time for Rejoicing 126

A Personal Letter
From the Author

Dear FRIEND,

Perhaps I am more or less of a stranger to you. But, in sorrow and tragedy, THERE ARE NO STRANGERS, and so I am reaching out my hand to you in deep and understanding sympathy.

I know the "heart—hurt" and "lost—loneliness" you are experiencing. But, after the first, stabbing anguish of grief has been softened by time, you will find great comfort in knowing that "our loved ones" are safe and free from all tears, trials, troubles, and temptations, for now they are WHERE NOTHING CAN EVER HURT THEM AGAIN!

Parting from our loved ones is something that we cannot escape, and death is just as it should be . . . WE ARE, and then WE ARE NOT. It is like the blowing out of a candle or the closing of a door. We go to sleep so that we may awaken in the morning, and if we did not sleep, we could never know the joy of awakening. And if we did not die, we could never LIVE ETERNALLY.

Always remember, our loved ones just go beyond the sight of our vision and the touch of our hands, and they are waiting for us "ON THE OTHER SIDE OF DEATH" . . . WHERE TIME IS NOT COUNTED BY YEARS and THERE ARE NO SEPARATIONS!

I have always felt, at times like this, there is so little anyone can say, for there are no words that have ever been invented to fit the loss of a loved one. But in death we find that we are drawn closer to one another and to GOD, and HEAVEN seems a little NEARER, GOD'S PROMISE a little CLEARER, and HIS LOVE a little DEARER.

We give our loved ones back to GOD. And just as HE first GAVE them to us and did not lose them in the GIVING, so we have not lost them in RETURNING them to HIM . . . for LIFE is ETERNAL, LOVE is IMMORTAL, DEATH is only a HORIZON, and a HORIZON is nothing but THE LIMIT OF OUR EARTHLY SIGHT.

In the poems of this book, I am trying to say that, in THE KINGDOM of THE LORD, THERE IS NOTHING LOST FOREVER . . . for, if we believe GOD'S PROMISE and doubt HIS GOODNESS never, we will meet all those who left us . . . to be TOGETHER in THE KINGDOM of FOREVER!

"LOVINGLY and PRAYERFULLY,"

Life Is Forever

Nothing on Earth
Is Forever Yours—
Only the Love of
the Lord Endures!

Everything in life is passing
            and whatever we possess
Cannot endure forever
            but ends in nothingness,
For there are no safety boxes
            nor vaults that can contain
The possessions we collected
            and desire to retain . . .
So all that man acquires,
            be it power, fame or jewels,
Is but limited and earthly,
            only "treasure made for fools" . . .
For only in GOD'S KINGDOM
            can man find enduring treasure,
Priceless gifts of love and beauty—
            more than mortal man can measure,
And the "riches" he accumulates
            he can keep and part with never,

For only in GOD'S KINGDOM
       do our treasures last FOREVER . . .
So use the word FOREVER
       with sanctity and love,
For NOTHING IS FOREVER
       BUT THE LOVE OF GOD ABOVE!

KINGS and KINGDOMS
       ALL PASS AWAY—
NOTHING ON EARTH ENDURES . . .
But THE LOVE of GOD
       WHO SENT HIS SON
IS FOREVER and EVER YOURS!

Life Is Forever: Death Is a Dream!

If we did not go to sleep at night
We'd never awaken to see the light,
And the joy of watching a new day break
Or meeting the dawn by some quiet lake
Would never be ours unless we slept
While God and all His angels kept
A vigil through this "little death"
That's over with the morning's breath—
And death, too, is a time of sleeping,
For those who die are in God's keeping
And there's a "sunrise" for each soul,
For LIFE, not DEATH, is God's promised
      goal—
So trust God's promise and doubt Him never
For only through death can man LIVE
      FOREVER!

I Do Not Go Alone

If DEATH should beckon me with out-
      stretched hand
And whisper softly of "AN UNKNOWN
      LAND,"
I shall not be afraid to go,
For though the path I do not know,
I take DEATH'S HAND without a fear,
For He who safely brought me here
Will also take me safely back,
And though in many things I lack,
He will not let me go alone
Into the "VALLEY THAT'S UN-
      KNOWN" . . .
So I reach out and take DEATH'S HAND
And journey to the "PROMISED LAND!"

Spring Awakens
What Autumn Puts to Sleep

A garden of asters of varying hues,
Crimson-pinks and violet-blues,
Blossoming in the hazy Fall
Wrapped in Autumn's lazy pall—
But early frost stole in one night
And like a chilling, killing blight
It touched each pretty aster's head
And now the garden's still and dead
And all the lovely flowers that bloomed
Will soon be buried and entombed
In Winter's icy shroud of snow
But oh, how wonderful to know
That after Winter comes the Spring
To breathe new life in everything,
And all the flowers that fell in death
Will be awakened by Spring's breath—
For in God's Plan both men and flowers
Can only reach "bright, shining hours"
By dying first to rise in glory
And prove again the Easter Story.

Death Is a Doorway

On the "WINGS of DEATH"
      the "SOUL takes FLIGHT"
Into the land where
      "THERE IS NO NIGHT"—
For those who believe
      what the Saviour said
Will rise in glory
      though they be dead . . .
So death comes to us
      just to "OPEN THE DOOR"
To the KINGDOM OF GOD
      and LIFE EVERMORE.

Every mile we walk in SORROW
Brings us NEARER to God's TOMORROW!

There's Always a Springtime

After the Winter comes the Spring
To show us again that in everything
There's always renewal divinely planned,
Flawlessly perfect, the work of God's
      Hand . . .
And just like the seasons that come and go
When the flowers of Spring lay buried in
      snow,
God sends to the heart in its winter of sadness
A springtime awakening of new hope and
      gladness,
And loved ones who sleep in a season of death
Will, too, be awakened by God's life-giving
      breath.

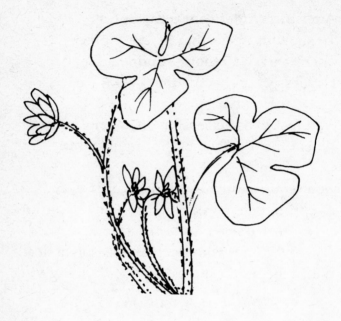

All who believe
in God's mercy and grace
Will meet their loved ones
face to face
Where time is endless
and joy unbroken
And only the words
of God's love are spoken.

"Because He Lives . . .
We, Too, Shall Live"

In this restless world of struggle
      it is very hard to find
Answers to the questions
      that daily come to mind—
We cannot see the future,
      what's beyond is still unknown,
For the secret of God's Kingdom
      still belongs to Him alone—
But He granted us salvation
      when His Son was crucified,
For life became immortal
      because our Saviour died.

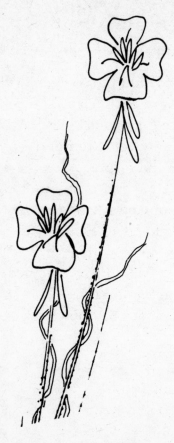

Life is not a transient thing—
It is *CHANGE* but never *LOSS*,
For Christ purchased our salvation
When He died upon THE CROSS!

When I Must Leave You

When I must leave you
        for a little while,
Please do not grieve
        and shed wild tears
And hug your sorrow
        to you through the years,
But start out bravely
        with a gallant smile;
And for my sake
        and in my name
Live on and do
        all things the same,
Feed not your loneliness
        on empty days,
But fill each waking hour
        in useful ways,
Reach out your hand
        in comfort and in cheer
And I in turn will comfort you
        and hold you near;
And never, never
        be afraid to die,
For I am waiting
        for you in the sky!

We part with our loved ones
  but not forever
If we trust God's promise
  and doubt it never!

Each Spring,
God Renews His Promise

Long, long ago in a land far away,
There came the dawn of the first Easter Day,
And each year we see that promise reborn
That God gave the world on that first Easter
      Morn . . .
For in each waking flower and each singing
      bird,
The Promise of Easter is witnessed and heard,
And Spring is God's way of speaking to men
And renewing the promise of Easter again,
For death is a season that man must pass
      through
And, just like the flowers, God wakens him,
      too . . .
So why should we grieve when our loved ones
      die,
For we'll meet them again in a "cloudless
      sky"—
For Easter is more than a beautiful story,
It's the promise of life and Eternal Glory.

Death "bursts our chrysalis of clay"
     so that our soul is free
To soar toward ETERNITY
     to dwell in PEACE with THEE!

Death Is Only a Part of Life

We enter this world
        from "THE GREAT UNKNOWN"
And GOD gives each SPIRIT
        a form of its own
And endows this form
        with a heart and a soul
To spur man on
        to his ultimate goal . . .
For all men are born
        to RETURN as they CAME
And birth and death
        are in essence the same
And man is but born
        to die and arise
For beyond this world
        in beauty there lies
The purpose of death
        which is but to gain
LIFE EVERLASTING
        in GOD'S GREAT DOMAIN . . .
And no one need make
        this journey alone
For GOD has promised
        to take care of HIS own.

LIVE for "ME"
And DIE for "ME"
And I, THY GOD,
Will set you FREE!

On the Other Side of Death

Death is a GATEWAY
        we all must past through
To reach that Fair Land
        where the soul's born anew,
For man's born to die
        and his sojourn on earth
Is a short span of years
        beginning with birth . . .
And like pilgrims we wander
        until death takes our hand
And we start on our journey
        to God's Promised Land,
A place where we'll find
        no suffering nor tears,
Where TIME is not counted
        by days, months or years . . .
And in this Fair City
        that God has prepared
Are unending joys
        to be happily shared
With all of our loved ones
        who patiently wait
On Death's Other Side
        to open "THE GATE"!

[105]

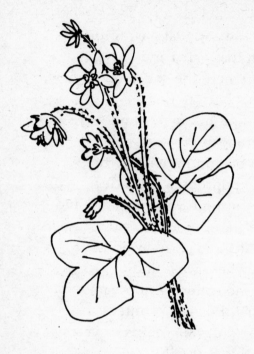

When DEATH STEPS IN,
        NEW LIFE BEGINS
And we rise above
        our temptations and sins!

Death Opens the Door to Life Evermore

We live a short while on earth below,
Reluctant to die for we do not know
Just what "dark death" is all about
And so we view it with fear and doubt
Not certain of what is around the bend
We look on death as the final end
To all that made us a mortal being
And yet there lies just beyond our seeing
A beautiful life so full and complete
That we should leave with hurrying feet
To walk with God by sacred streams
Amid beauty and peace beyond our dreams—
For all who believe in the RISEN LORD
Have been assured of this reward
And death for them is just "graduation"
To a higher realm of wide elevation—
For life on earth is a transient affair,
Just a few brief years in which to prepare
For a life that is free from pain and tears
Where time is not counted by hours or years—
For death is only the method God chose
To colonize heaven with the souls of those

Who by their apprenticeship on earth
Proved worthy to dwell in the land of new
     birth—
So death is not sad . . . it's a time of elation,
A joyous transition . . . the soul's emigra-
     tion
Into a place where the soul's SAFE and FREE
To live with God through ETERNITY!

Life Is Eternal

"LIFE IS ETERNAL," the GOOD LORD said,
So do not think of your loved one as dead—
For death is only a stepping stone
To a beautiful life we have never known,
A place where GOD promised man he would
        be
Eternally happy and safe and free,
A wonderful land where we live anew
When our journey on earth is over and
        through—
So trust in GOD and doubt HIM never
For all who love HIM live forever,
And while we cannot understand
Just let the SAVIOUR take your hand,
For when DEATH'S ANGEL comes to call
"GOD is so GREAT and we're so small" . . .
And there is nothing you need fear
For FAITH IN GOD makes all things clear.

"In Him We Live and Move and Have Our Being"

We walk in a world that is strange and unknown
And in the midst of the crowd we still feel alone,
We question our purpose, our part and our place
In this vast land of mystery suspended in space,
We probe and explore and try hard to explain
The tumult of thoughts that our minds
        entertain . . .
But all of our probings and complex explanations
Of man's inner feelings and fears and frustrations
Still leave us engulfed in the "MYSTERY of LIFE"
With all of its struggles and suffering and strife,
Unable to fathom what tomorrow will bring—
But there is one truth to which we can cling,
For while LIFE'S a MYSTERY man can't under-
        stand
The "GREAT GIVER of LIFE" is holding our hand
And safe in HIS care there is no need for seeing
For "IN HIM WE LIVE and MOVE and HAVE OUR
        BEING."

In God's Tomorrow
There Is Eternal Spring

All nature heeds the call of Spring
As GOD awakens everything,
And all that seemed so dead and still
Experiences a sudden thrill
As Springtime lays a magic hand
Across GOD'S vast and fertile land—
Oh, how can anyone stand by
And watch a sapphire Springtime sky
Or see a fragile flower break through
What just a day ago or two
Seemed barren ground still hard with frost,
But in GOD'S world no life is lost,
And flowers sleep beneath the ground
But when they hear Spring's waking sound
They push themselves through layers of clay
To reach the sunlight of GOD'S DAY—
And man, like flowers, too, must sleep
Until he is called from the "darkened deep"
To live in that place where angels sing
And where there is ETERNAL SPRING!

God Needed an Angel in Heaven

When JESUS lived upon the earth
      so many years ago,
HE called the children close to HIM
      because HE loved them so . . .
And with the tenderness of old,
      that same sweet, gentle way,
HE holds your little loved one close
      within HIS ARMS today . . .
And you'll find comfort in your faith
      that in HIS HOME ABOVE
The GOD of little children
      gives your little one HIS LOVE . . .
So think of your little darling
      lighthearted and happy and free
Playing in GOD'S PROMISED LAND
      where there is JOY ETERNALLY.

The Tiny "Rosebud" God Picked to Bloom in Heaven

THE MASTER GARDENER
From HEAVEN ABOVE
Planted a seed
In THE GARDEN of LOVE
And from it there grew
A rosebud small
That never had time
To open at all,
For GOD in HIS perfect
And all-wise way
Chose this rose
For HIS HEAVENLY BOUQUET
And great was the joy
Of this tiny rose
To be the one our FATHER chose
To leave earth's garden
For ONE on high
Where roses bloom always
And never die . . .
So, while you can't see

[113]

Your precious rose bloom,
You know THE GREAT GARDENER
From the "UPPER ROOM"
Is watching and tending
This wee rose with care,
Tenderly touching
Each petal so fair . . .
So think of your darling
With the angels above
Secure and contented
And surrounded by love,
And remember GOD blessed
And enriched your lives, too,
For in dying your darling
Brought HEAVEN CLOSER TO YOU!

Mothers Never Die—
They Just Keep House
up in the Sky

When we are children, we are happy and gay
And our MOTHER is young and she laughs as
      we play,
Then as we grow up, she teaches us truth
And lays life's foundation in the days of our
      youth—
And then it is time for us to leave home
But her teachings go with us wherever we
      roam,
For all that she taught us and all that we did
When we were so often just a "bad, little kid"
We will often remember and then realize
That MOTHERS ARE SPECIAL and WON-
      DERFULLY WISE . . .
And as she grows older, we look back with
      love
Knowing that MOTHERS ARE "GIFTS FROM
      ABOVE,"
And when she "goes home" to receive her re-
      ward

She will dwell in GOD'S KINGDOM and
   · "KEEP HOUSE for THE LORD"
Where she'll "light up" the stars that shine
   through the night
And keep all the moonbeams "sparkling and
   bright"
And then with the dawn she'll put the dark-
   ness away
As she "scours" the sun to new brilliance each
   day . . .
So dry tears of sorrow, for MOTHERS DON'T
   DIE—
They just move in with GOD and "KEEP
   HOUSE IN THE SKY,"
And there in GOD'S KINGDOM, MOTHERS
   watch from above
To welcome their children with their UNDY-
   ING LOVE!

"Why Should He Die for Such as I?"

In everything both great and small
We see the HAND of GOD in all,
And in the MIRACLES of Spring
When EVERYWHERE in EVERYTHING
HIS HANDIWORK is all around
And every lovely sight and sound
Proclaims the GOD of earth and sky
I ask myself JUST WHO AM I
That GOD should send HIS ONLY SON
That my salvation would be won
Upon a CROSS by a SINLESS MAN
To bring fulfillment to GOD'S PLAN—
For JESUS suffered, bled and died
That sinners might be sanctified,
And to grant GOD'S children such as I
ETERNAL LIFE in that HOME ON HIGH.

HEAVEN is REAL—
      IT'S a "POSITIVE PLACE"
Where those who believe
      MEET GOD FACE TO FACE!

[118]

"I Know That My Redeemer Liveth"

They asked me how I know it's true
That the Saviour lived and died . . .
And if I believe the story
That the Lord was crucified?
And I have so many answers
To prove His Holy Being,
Answers that are everywhere
Within the realm of seeing . . .
The leaves that fell at Autumn
And were buried in the sod
Now budding on the tree boughs
To lift their arms to God . . .
The flowers that were covered
And entombed beneath the snow
Pushing through the "darkness"
To bid the Spring "hello" . . .
On every side Great Nature
Retells the Easter Story—
So who am I to question
"The Resurrection Glory."

All Nature Proclaims Eternal Life

Flowers sleeping 'neath the snow,
Awakening when the Spring winds blow;
Leafless trees so bare before,
Gowned in lacy green once more;
Hard, unyielding, frozen sod
Now softly carpeted by GOD;
Still streams melting in the Spring,
Rippling over rocks that sing;
Barren, windswept, lonely hills
Turning gold with daffodils . . .
These MIRACLES are all around
Within our sight and touch and sound,
As true and wonderful today
As when "the stone was rolled away"
Proclaiming to all doubting men
That in GOD all things live again.

"I Am the Way, the Truth, and the Life"

I AM THE WAY
       so just follow ME
Though the way be rough
       and you cannot see . . .

I AM THE TRUTH
       which all men seek
So heed not "false prophets"
       nor the words that they speak . . .

I AM THE LIFE
       and I hold the key
That opens the door
       to ETERNITY . . .

And in this dark world
       I AM THE LIGHT
To THE PROMISED LAND
       WHERE THERE IS NO NIGHT!

The Legend of the Raindrop

The legend of the raindrop
        has a lesson for us all
As it trembled in the heavens
        questioning whether it should fall—
For the glistening raindrop argued
        to the genie of the sky,
"I am beautiful and lovely
        as I sparkle here on high,
And hanging here I will become
        part of the rainbow's hue
And I'll shimmer like a diamond
        for all the world to view" . . .
But the genie told the raindrop,
        "Do not hesitate to go,
For you will be more beautiful
        if you fall to earth below,
For you will sink into the soil
        and be lost a while from sight,
But when you reappear on earth,
        you'll be looked on with delight;
For you will be the raindrop
        that quenched the thirsty ground
And helped the lovely flowers
        to blossom all around

And in your resurrection
        you'll appear in queenly clothes
With the beauty of the lily
        and the fragrance of the rose;
Then, when you wilt and wither,
        you'll become part of the earth
And make the soil more fertile
        and give new flowers birth" . . .
For there is nothing ever lost
        or ETERNALLY NEGLECTED,
For EVERYTHING GOD EVER MADE
        IS ALWAYS RESURRECTED;
So trust God's all-wise wisdom
        and doubt the Father never,
For in HIS HEAVENLY KINGDOM
        THERE IS NOTHING LOST
        FOREVER.

As Long As You Live
and Remember—
Your Loved One
Lives in Your Heart!

May tender memories
          soften your grief,
May fond recollection
          bring you relief,
And may you find comfort
          and peace in the thought
Of the joy that knowing
          your loved one brought—
For time and space
          can never divide
Or keep your loved one
          from your side
When memory paints
          in colors true
The happy hours
          that belonged to you.

A Consolation Meditation

On the wings
　　of death and sorrow
God sends us
　　new hope for tomorrow—
And in His mercy
　　and His grace
He gives us strength
　　to bravely face
The lonely days
　　that stretch ahead
And know our loved one
　　is not dead
But only sleeping
　　and out of our sight
And we'll meet in that land
　　WHERE THERE IS NO NIGHT.

In the Hands of God Even Death Is a Time for Rejoicing

And so when death brings weeping
    and the heart is filled with sorrow,
It beckons us to seek GOD
    as we ask about "TOMORROW" . . .
And in these hours of "heart-hurt"
    we draw closer to believing
That even death in GOD'S HANDS
    is not a cause for grieving
But a time for joy in knowing
    death is just a stepping-stone
To a LIFE that's EVERLASTING
    such as we have never known.

Index of Titles
and First Lines

After the Winter comes the Spring 95

*As Long As You Live and Remember—Your
   Loved One Lives in Your Heart!* 124

A garden of asters of varying hues 93

All nature heeds the call of Spring 111

All Nature Proclaims Eternal Life 120

All who believe 96

And so when death brings weeping 126

"Because He Lives . . . We, Too, Shall Live" 97

Consolation Meditation, A 125

Death "bursts our chrysalis of clay" 102

Death Is a Doorway 94

Death is a gateway 105

Death Is Only a Part of Life 103

Death Opens the Door to Life Evermore 107

Each Spring, God Renews His Promise 101

Everything in life is passing 89

Flowers sleeping 'neath the snow 120

God Needed an Angel in Heaven 112

Heaven is real 118

I am the Way 121

"I Am the Way, the Truth, and the Life" 121

I Do Not Go Alone 92

If death should beckon me with out-
   stretched hand 92

If we did not go to sleep at night 91

"I Know That My Redeemer Liveth" 119

In everything both great and small 117

In God's Tomorrow There Is Eternal Spring 111

*"In Him We Live and Move and Have Our
   Being"* 110

*In The Hands of God, Even Death Is a Time for
   Rejoicing* 126

In this restless world of struggle   97
Kings and kingdoms all pass away   92

Legend of the Raindrop, The   122
Life Is Eternal   109
"Life is Eternal," the good Lord said   109
Life Is Forever: Death Is a Dream!   91
Life is not a transient thing   98
Live for "Me"   104
Long, long ago in a land far away   101

May tender memories soften your grief   124
Mothers Never Die   115

*Nothing on Earth Is Forever Yours—Only the
    Love of the Lord Endures!*   89

On the Other Side of Death   105
On the "wings of death"   94
On the wings of death and sorrow   125

Spring Awakens What Autumn Puts to Sleep   93

The legend of the raindrop   122
The Master Gardener from heaven above   113
There's Always a Springtime   95
*The Tiny "Rosebud" God Picked to Bloom
    in Heaven*   113
They asked me how I know it's true   119

We enter this world from "the great
    unknown"   103
We live a short while on earth below   107
We part with our loved ones   100
We walk in a world that is strange and
    unknown   110
When death steps in   106
When I Must Leave You   99
When I must leave you   99
When Jesus lived upon the earth   112
When we are children, we are happy and gay   115
"Why Should He Die for Such as I?"   117